Travel Journal

go where you feel most alive

Let's go travel

TRAVEL Bucket List

PLACES I WANT TO VISIT:

THINGS I WANT TO SEE:

TOP 3 DESTINATIONS:

TRIP Itinerary

DESTINATION: DATE:

MON

TUE

WED

THU

FRI

SAT

SUN

travel
is
always
a good
IDEA

TRAVEL Information

HOTEL INFORMATION

NAME OF HOTEL:

ADDRESS:

PHONE NUMBER:

CONFIRMATION #:

RATE PER NIGHT:

FLIGHT INFORMATION

AIRLINE:

LOCATION:

FLIGHT #:

CHECK IN TIME:

DEPARTURE TIME:

REFERENCE #:

NOTES

TRAVEL Information

<table>
<tr><td rowspan="5">CAR RENTAL INFORMATION</td><td>COMPANY:</td></tr>
<tr><td>ADDRESS:</td></tr>
<tr><td>PHONE NUMBER:</td></tr>
<tr><td>CONFIRMATION #:</td></tr>
<tr><td>TOTAL COST:</td></tr>
</table>

<table>
<tr><td rowspan="5">EVENT INFORMATION</td><td>EVENT NAME:</td></tr>
<tr><td>LOCATION:</td></tr>
<tr><td>PHONE NUMBER:</td></tr>
<tr><td>START TIME:</td></tr>
<tr><td>OTHER:</td></tr>
</table>

NOTES

TRAVEL Information

HOTEL INFORMATION

NAME OF HOTEL:

ADDRESS:

PHONE NUMBER:

CONFIRMATION #:

RATE PER NIGHT:

FLIGHT INFORMATION

AIRLINE:

LOCATION:

FLIGHT #:

CHECK IN TIME:

DEPARTURE TIME:

REFERENCE #:

NOTES

Bon
Voyage

TRAVEL Planner

PRE-TRAVEL CHECKLIST

1 MONTH BEFORE	2 WEEKS BEFORE
☐	☐
☐	☐
☐	☐
☐	☐
☐	☐

1 WEEK BEFORE	2 DAYS BEFORE
☐	☐
☐	☐
☐	☐
☐	☐
☐	☐

24 HOURS BEFORE	DAY OF TRAVEL
☐	☐
☐	☐
☐	☐
☐	☐

TRIP TO DO LIST Countdown

travel addict

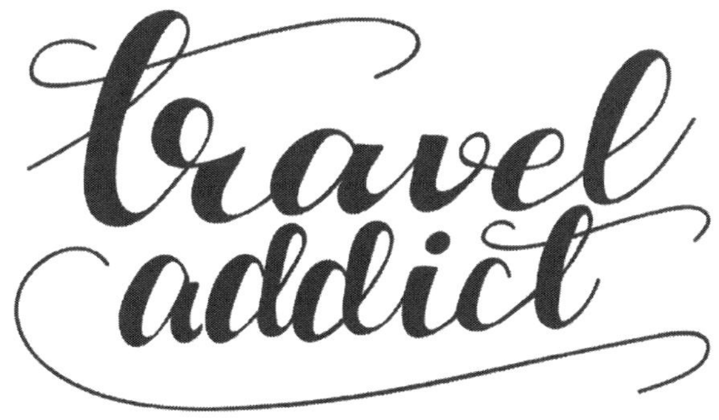

OUTFIT Planner

DAY: **DESTINATION:** **PACKED:** ☐

DAY:

ACTIVITY: _______________ **EVENING:**

OUTFIT: _______________

SHOES: _______________

ACC: _______________

DAY: **DESTINATION:** **PACKED:** ☐

DAY:

ACTIVITY: _______________ **EVENING:**

OUTFIT: _______________

SHOES: _______________

ACC: _______________

DAY: **DESTINATION:** **PACKED:** ☐

DAY:

ACTIVITY: _______________ **EVENING:**

OUTFIT: _______________

SHOES: _______________

ACC: _______________

exiting

ADVENTURE

PACKING Check List

DOCUMENTS

- [ ] PASSPORT
- [ ] DRIVER'S LICENSE
- [ ] VISA
- [ ] PLANE TICKETS
- [ ] LOCAL CURRENCY
- [ ] INSURANCE CARD
- [ ] HEALTH CARD
- [ ] OTHER ID
- [ ] HOTEL INFORMATION
- [ ] _______________
- [ ] _______________

CLOTHING

- [ ] UNDERWEAR / SOCKS
- [ ] SWIM WEAR
- [ ] T-SHIRTS
- [ ] JEANS/PANTS
- [ ] SHORTS
- [ ] SKIRTS / DRESSES
- [ ] JACKET / COAT
- [ ] SLEEPWEAR
- [ ] SHOES
- [ ] _______________
- [ ] _______________

PERSONAL ITEMS

- [ ] SHAMPOO
- [ ] RAZORS
- [ ] COSMETICS
- [ ] HAIR BRUSH
- [ ] LIP BALM
- [ ] WATER BOTTLE
- [ ] SOAP
- [ ] TOOTHBRUSH
- [ ] JEWELRY
- [ ] _______________
- [ ] _______________

ELECTRONICS

- [ ] CELL PHONE
- [ ] CHARGER
- [ ] LAPTOP
- [ ] BATTERIES
- [ ] EARPHONES
- [ ] FLASH DRIVE
- [ ] MEMORY CARD
- [ ] _______________
- [ ] _______________
- [ ] _______________

HEALTH & SAFETY

- [ ] HAND SANITIZER
- [ ] SUNSCREEN
- [ ] VITAMIN SUPPLEMENTS
- [ ] BANDAIDS
- [ ] ADVIL/TYLENOL
- [ ] CONTACTS / GLASSES
- [ ] COLD/FLU MEDS
- [ ] _______________
- [ ] _______________
- [ ] _______________

OTHER ESSENTIALS

- [ ] _______________
- [ ] _______________
- [ ] _______________
- [ ] _______________
- [ ] _______________
- [ ] _______________
- [ ] _______________
- [ ] _______________
- [ ] _______________
- [ ] _______________

PACKING Check List

OUTWARD Journey Schedule

DATE:

DAY:

6

7

8

9

10

11

12

1

2

3

4

5

6

7

8

9

10

11

12

NOTES

REMINDERS

Let's
TRAVEL
THE
World

DAILY Travel Planner

<table>
<tr><td>DATE:</td><td>ATTRACTION:</td><td>THINGS TO SEE</td></tr>
</table>

<table>
<tr><td>DATE:</td><td>ATTRACTION:</td><td>THINGS TO SEE</td></tr>
</table>

DAILY Travel Planner

DATE:	ATTRACTION:	THINGS TO SEE

DATE:	ATTRACTION:	THINGS TO SEE

Travel Expense Tracker

DESTINATION: _______________________   BUDGET GOAL: _______________________

DATE:	DESCRIPTION:	CURRENCY:	AMOUNT:

TOTAL EXPENSES:

Enjoy
every
moment

Daily TRAVEL JOURNAL

MON

TUE

WED

THU

Daily TRAVEL JOURNAL

FRI

SAT

SUN

RETURN Journey Schedule

DATE:

DAY:

6

7

8

9

10

11

12

1

2

3

4

5

6

7

8

9

10

11

12

NOTES

REMINDERS

Let's go travel

TRAVEL Bucket List

PLACES I WANT TO VISIT:

THINGS I WANT TO SEE:

TOP 3 DESTINATIONS:

TRIP Itinerary

DESTINATION: DATE:

MON

TUE

WED

THU

FRI

SAT

SUN

travel
is
always
a good
IDEA

TRAVEL Information

HOTEL INFORMATION

NAME OF HOTEL:

ADDRESS:

PHONE NUMBER:

CONFIRMATION #:

RATE PER NIGHT:

FLIGHT INFORMATION

AIRLINE:

LOCATION:

FLIGHT #:

CHECK IN TIME:

DEPARTURE TIME:

REFERENCE #:

NOTES

TRAVEL Information

CAR RENTAL INFORMATION

COMPANY:

ADDRESS:

PHONE NUMBER:

CONFIRMATION #:

TOTAL COST:

EVENT INFORMATION

EVENT NAME:

LOCATION:

PHONE NUMBER:

START TIME:

OTHER:

NOTES

TRAVEL Information

NAME OF HOTEL:

ADDRESS:

PHONE NUMBER:

CONFIRMATION #:

RATE PER NIGHT:

AIRLINE:

LOCATION:

FLIGHT #:

CHECK IN TIME:

DEPARTURE TIME:

REFERENCE #:

NOTES

Bon
Voyage

TRAVEL Planner

PRE-TRAVEL CHECKLIST

1 MONTH BEFORE

- [ ]
- [ ]
- [ ]
- [ ]
- [ ]

2 WEEKS BEFORE

- [ ]
- [ ]
- [ ]
- [ ]
- [ ]

1 WEEK BEFORE

- [ ]
- [ ]
- [ ]
- [ ]
- [ ]

2 DAYS BEFORE

- [ ]
- [ ]
- [ ]
- [ ]
- [ ]

24 HOURS BEFORE

- [ ]
- [ ]
- [ ]
- [ ]

DAY OF TRAVEL

- [ ]
- [ ]
- [ ]
- [ ]

TRIP TO DO LIST Countdown

- [ ]
- [ ]
- [ ]
- [ ]
- [ ]
- [ ]
- [ ]
- [ ]
- [ ]

travel addict

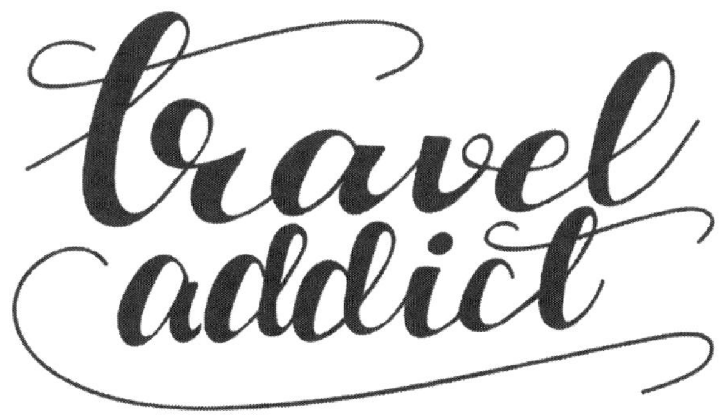

OUTFIT Planner

<table>
<tr><td>DAY:</td><td>DESTINATION:</td><td>PACKED:</td><td>☐</td></tr>
</table>

DAY:

ACTIVITY: ___________

OUTFIT: ___________

SHOES: ___________

ACC: ___________

EVENING:

<table>
<tr><td>DAY:</td><td>DESTINATION:</td><td>PACKED:</td><td>☐</td></tr>
</table>

DAY:

ACTIVITY: ___________

OUTFIT: ___________

SHOES: ___________

ACC: ___________

EVENING:

<table>
<tr><td>DAY:</td><td>DESTINATION:</td><td>PACKED:</td><td>☐</td></tr>
</table>

DAY:

ACTIVITY: ___________

OUTFIT: ___________

SHOES: ___________

ACC: ___________

EVENING:

exiting
ADVENTURE

PACKING Check List

DOCUMENTS

- [ ] PASSPORT
- [ ] DRIVER'S LICENSE
- [ ] VISA
- [ ] PLANE TICKETS
- [ ] LOCAL CURRENCY
- [ ] INSURANCE CARD
- [ ] HEALTH CARD
- [ ] OTHER ID
- [ ] HOTEL INFORMATION
- [ ] ______________
- [ ] ______________

CLOTHING

- [ ] UNDERWEAR / SOCKS
- [ ] SWIM WEAR
- [ ] T-SHIRTS
- [ ] JEANS/PANTS
- [ ] SHORTS
- [ ] SKIRTS / DRESSES
- [ ] JACKET / COAT
- [ ] SLEEPWEAR
- [ ] SHOES
- [ ] ______________
- [ ] ______________

PERSONAL ITEMS

- [ ] SHAMPOO
- [ ] RAZORS
- [ ] COSMETICS
- [ ] HAIR BRUSH
- [ ] LIP BALM
- [ ] WATER BOTTLE
- [ ] SOAP
- [ ] TOOTHBRUSH
- [ ] JEWELRY
- [ ] ______________
- [ ] ______________

ELECTRONICS

- [ ] CELL PHONE
- [ ] CHARGER
- [ ] LAPTOP
- [ ] BATTERIES
- [ ] EARPHONES
- [ ] FLASH DRIVE
- [ ] MEMORY CARD
- [ ] ______________
- [ ] ______________
- [ ] ______________

HEALTH & SAFETY

- [ ] HAND SANITIZER
- [ ] SUNSCREEN
- [ ] VITAMIN SUPPLEMENTS
- [ ] BANDAIDS
- [ ] ADVIL/TYLENOL
- [ ] CONTACTS / GLASSES
- [ ] COLD/FLU MEDS
- [ ] ______________
- [ ] ______________
- [ ] ______________

OTHER ESSENTIALS

- [ ] ______________
- [ ] ______________
- [ ] ______________
- [ ] ______________
- [ ] ______________
- [ ] ______________
- [ ] ______________
- [ ] ______________
- [ ] ______________

PACKING Check List

OUTWARD Journey Schedule

DATE:

DAY:

NOTES

REMINDERS

6

7

8

9

10

11

12

1

2

3

4

5

6

7

8

9

10

11

12

Let's
TRAVEL
THE
World

DAILY Travel Planner

DATE:	ATTRACTION:	THINGS TO SEE

DATE:	ATTRACTION:	THINGS TO SEE

DAILY Travel Planner

DATE:	ATTRACTION:	THINGS TO SEE

DATE:	ATTRACTION:	THINGS TO SEE

Travel Expense Tracker

DESTINATION: _______________   BUDGET GOAL: _______________

DATE:	DESCRIPTION:	CURRENCY:	AMOUNT:

TOTAL EXPENSES:

Enjoy
every
moment

Daily TRAVEL JOURNAL

MON

TUE

WED

THU

Daily TRAVEL JOURNAL

FRI

SAT

SUN

RETURN Journey Schedule

6

7

8

9

10

11

12

1

2

3

4

5

6

7

8

9

10

11

12

NOTES

REMINDERS

Let's go
travel

TRAVEL Bucket List

PLACES I WANT TO VISIT:

THINGS I WANT TO SEE:

TOP 3 DESTINATIONS:

TRIP Itinerary

<table>
<tr><td>DESTINATION:</td><td>DATE:</td></tr>
</table>

MON

TUE

WED

THU

FRI

SAT

SUN

travel
is
always
a good
IDEA

TRAVEL Information

HOTEL INFORMATION

NAME OF HOTEL:

ADDRESS:

PHONE NUMBER:

CONFIRMATION #:

RATE PER NIGHT:

FLIGHT INFORMATION

AIRLINE:

LOCATION:

FLIGHT #:

CHECK IN TIME:

DEPARTURE TIME:

REFERENCE #:

NOTES

TRAVEL Information

CAR RENTAL INFORMATION

COMPANY:

ADDRESS:

PHONE NUMBER:

CONFIRMATION #:

TOTAL COST:

EVENT INFORMATION

EVENT NAME:

LOCATION:

PHONE NUMBER:

START TIME:

OTHER:

NOTES

TRAVEL Information

<table>
<tr><td rowspan="5">HOTEL INFORMATION</td><td>NAME OF HOTEL:</td></tr>
<tr><td>ADDRESS:</td></tr>
<tr><td>PHONE NUMBER:</td></tr>
<tr><td>CONFIRMATION #:</td></tr>
<tr><td>RATE PER NIGHT:</td></tr>
</table>

<table>
<tr><td rowspan="6">FLIGHT INFORMATION</td><td>AIRLINE:</td></tr>
<tr><td>LOCATION:</td></tr>
<tr><td>FLIGHT #:</td></tr>
<tr><td>CHECK IN TIME:</td></tr>
<tr><td>DEPARTURE TIME:</td></tr>
<tr><td>REFERENCE #:</td></tr>
</table>

NOTES

Bon Voyage

TRAVEL Planner

PRE-TRAVEL CHECKLIST

1 MONTH BEFORE	2 WEEKS BEFORE
☐	☐
☐	☐
☐	☐
☐	☐
☐	☐

1 WEEK BEFORE	2 DAYS BEFORE
☐	☐
☐	☐
☐	☐
☐	☐

24 HOURS BEFORE	DAY OF TRAVEL
☐	☐
☐	☐
☐	☐
☐	☐

TRIP TO DO LIST Countdown

OUTFIT Planner

DAY:	DESTINATION:	PACKED:

DAY:

EVENING:

ACTIVITY:

OUTFIT:

SHOES:

ACC:

DAY:	DESTINATION:	PACKED:

DAY:

EVENING:

ACTIVITY:

OUTFIT:

SHOES:

ACC:

DAY:	DESTINATION:	PACKED:

DAY:

EVENING:

ACTIVITY:

OUTFIT:

SHOES:

ACC:

exiting
ADVENTURE

PACKING Check List

DOCUMENTS

- [ ] PASSPORT
- [ ] DRIVER'S LICENSE
- [ ] VISA
- [ ] PLANE TICKETS
- [ ] LOCAL CURRENCY
- [ ] INSURANCE CARD
- [ ] HEALTH CARD
- [ ] OTHER ID
- [ ] HOTEL INFORMATION
- [ ] _______________
- [ ] _______________

CLOTHING

- [ ] UNDERWEAR / SOCKS
- [ ] SWIM WEAR
- [ ] T-SHIRTS
- [ ] JEANS/PANTS
- [ ] SHORTS
- [ ] SKIRTS / DRESSES
- [ ] JACKET / COAT
- [ ] SLEEPWEAR
- [ ] SHOES
- [ ] _______________
- [ ] _______________

PERSONAL ITEMS

- [ ] SHAMPOO
- [ ] RAZORS
- [ ] COSMETICS
- [ ] HAIR BRUSH
- [ ] LIP BALM
- [ ] WATER BOTTLE
- [ ] SOAP
- [ ] TOOTHBRUSH
- [ ] JEWELRY
- [ ] _______________
- [ ] _______________

ELECTRONICS

- [ ] CELL PHONE
- [ ] CHARGER
- [ ] LAPTOP
- [ ] BATTERIES
- [ ] EARPHONES
- [ ] FLASH DRIVE
- [ ] MEMORY CARD
- [ ] _______________
- [ ] _______________
- [ ] _______________

HEALTH & SAFETY

- [ ] HAND SANITIZER
- [ ] SUNSCREEN
- [ ] VITAMIN SUPPLEMENTS
- [ ] BANDAIDS
- [ ] ADVIL/TYLENOL
- [ ] CONTACTS / GLASSES
- [ ] COLD/FLU MEDS
- [ ] _______________
- [ ] _______________
- [ ] _______________

OTHER ESSENTIALS

- [ ] _______________
- [ ] _______________
- [ ] _______________
- [ ] _______________
- [ ] _______________
- [ ] _______________
- [ ] _______________
- [ ] _______________
- [ ] _______________

PACKING Check List

OUTWARD Journey Schedule

DATE:

DAY:

6

7

8

9

10

11

12

1

2

3

4

5

6

7

8

9

10

11

12

NOTES

REMINDERS

Let's
TRAVEL
THE
World

DAILY Travel Planner

DATE:	ATTRACTION:

DATE:	ATTRACTION:

DAILY Travel Planner

DATE:	ATTRACTION:	THINGS TO SEE

DATE:	ATTRACTION:	THINGS TO SEE

Travel Expense Tracker

DESTINATION: _______________   BUDGET GOAL: _______________

DATE:	DESCRIPTION:	CURRENCY:	AMOUNT:

TOTAL EXPENSES:

Enjoy
every
moment

Daily TRAVEL JOURNAL

MON

TUE

WED

THU

Daily TRAVEL JOURNAL

FRI

SAT

SUN

RETURN Journey Schedule

6

7

8

9

10

11

12

1

2

3

4

5

6

7

8

9

10

11

12

Let's go
travel

TRAVEL Bucket List

PLACES I WANT TO VISIT:

THINGS I WANT TO SEE:

TOP 3 DESTINATIONS:

TRIP Itinerary

DESTINATION: DATE:

MON

TUE

WED

THU

FRI

SAT

SUN

travel
is
always
a good
IDEA

TRAVEL Information

<table>
<tr><td rowspan="7">HOTEL INFORMATION</td><td>NAME OF HOTEL:</td><td></td></tr>
<tr><td>ADDRESS:</td><td></td></tr>
<tr><td></td><td></td></tr>
<tr><td>PHONE NUMBER:</td><td></td></tr>
<tr><td>CONFIRMATION #:</td><td></td></tr>
<tr><td>RATE PER NIGHT:</td><td></td></tr>
</table>

<table>
<tr><td rowspan="6">FLIGHT INFORMATION</td><td>AIRLINE:</td><td></td></tr>
<tr><td>LOCATION:</td><td></td></tr>
<tr><td>FLIGHT #:</td><td></td></tr>
<tr><td>CHECK IN TIME:</td><td></td></tr>
<tr><td>DEPARTURE TIME:</td><td></td></tr>
<tr><td>REFERENCE #:</td><td></td></tr>
</table>

NOTES

TRAVEL Information

CAR RENTAL INFORMATION

COMPANY:

ADDRESS:

PHONE NUMBER:

CONFIRMATION #:

TOTAL COST:

EVENT INFORMATION

EVENT NAME:

LOCATION:

PHONE NUMBER:

START TIME:

OTHER:

NOTES

TRAVEL Information

NAME OF HOTEL:

ADDRESS:

PHONE NUMBER:

CONFIRMATION #:

RATE PER NIGHT:

AIRLINE:

LOCATION:

FLIGHT #:

CHECK IN TIME:

DEPARTURE TIME:

REFERENCE #:

NOTES

Bon Voyage

TRAVEL Planner

PRE-TRAVEL CHECKLIST

1 MONTH BEFORE	2 WEEKS BEFORE
☐	☐
☐	☐
☐	☐
☐	☐
☐	☐

1 WEEK BEFORE	2 DAYS BEFORE
☐	☐
☐	☐
☐	☐
☐	☐
☐	☐

24 HOURS BEFORE	DAY OF TRAVEL
☐	☐
☐	☐
☐	☐
☐	☐

TRIP TO DO LIST Countdown

OUTFIT Planner

DAY:	DESTINATION:	PACKED:

DAY: | **EVENING:**

ACTIVITY:

OUTFIT:

SHOES:

ACC:

DAY:	DESTINATION:	PACKED:

DAY: | **EVENING:**

ACTIVITY:

OUTFIT:

SHOES:

ACC:

DAY:	DESTINATION:	PACKED:

DAY: | **EVENING:**

ACTIVITY:

OUTFIT:

SHOES:

ACC:

exiting
ADVENTURE

PACKING Check List

DOCUMENTS

- [ ] PASSPORT
- [ ] DRIVER'S LICENSE
- [ ] VISA
- [ ] PLANE TICKETS
- [ ] LOCAL CURRENCY
- [ ] INSURANCE CARD
- [ ] HEALTH CARD
- [ ] OTHER ID
- [ ] HOTEL INFORMATION
- [ ] __________________
- [ ] __________________

CLOTHING

- [ ] UNDERWEAR / SOCKS
- [ ] SWIM WEAR
- [ ] T-SHIRTS
- [ ] JEANS/PANTS
- [ ] SHORTS
- [ ] SKIRTS / DRESSES
- [ ] JACKET / COAT
- [ ] SLEEPWEAR
- [ ] SHOES
- [ ] __________________
- [ ] __________________

PERSONAL ITEMS

- [ ] SHAMPOO
- [ ] RAZORS
- [ ] COSMETICS
- [ ] HAIR BRUSH
- [ ] LIP BALM
- [ ] WATER BOTTLE
- [ ] SOAP
- [ ] TOOTHBRUSH
- [ ] JEWELRY
- [ ] __________________
- [ ] __________________

ELECTRONICS

- [ ] CELL PHONE
- [ ] CHARGER
- [ ] LAPTOP
- [ ] BATTERIES
- [ ] EARPHONES
- [ ] FLASH DRIVE
- [ ] MEMORY CARD
- [ ] __________________
- [ ] __________________
- [ ] __________________

HEALTH & SAFETY

- [ ] HAND SANITIZER
- [ ] SUNSCREEN
- [ ] VITAMIN SUPPLEMENTS
- [ ] BANDAIDS
- [ ] ADVIL/TYLENOL
- [ ] CONTACTS / GLASSES
- [ ] COLD/FLU MEDS
- [ ] __________________
- [ ] __________________
- [ ] __________________

OTHER ESSENTIALS

- [ ] __________________
- [ ] __________________
- [ ] __________________
- [ ] __________________
- [ ] __________________
- [ ] __________________
- [ ] __________________
- [ ] __________________
- [ ] __________________
- [ ] __________________

PACKING Check List

OUTWARD Journey Schedule

DATE:

DAY:

6

7

8

9

10

11

12

1

2

3

4

5

6

7

8

9

10

11

12

NOTES

REMINDERS

Let's
TRAVEL
THE
World

DAILY Travel Planner

<table>
<tr><td>DATE:</td><td>ATTRACTION:</td><td>THINGS TO SEE</td></tr>
</table>

<table>
<tr><td>DATE:</td><td>ATTRACTION:</td><td>THINGS TO SEE</td></tr>
</table>

DAILY Travel Planner

DATE:	ATTRACTION:	THINGS TO SEE

DATE:	ATTRACTION:	THINGS TO SEE

Travel Expense Tracker

DESTINATION: __________________   BUDGET GOAL: __________________

DATE:	DESCRIPTION:	CURRENCY:	AMOUNT:

TOTAL EXPENSES:

Enjoy
every
moment

Daily TRAVEL JOURNAL

MON

TUE

WED

THU

Daily TRAVEL JOURNAL

FRI

SAT

SUN

RETURN Journey Schedule

Let's go
travel

Let's go
travel

TRAVEL Bucket List

PLACES I WANT TO VISIT:

THINGS I WANT TO SEE:

TOP 3 DESTINATIONS:

TRIP Itinerary

DESTINATION: DATE:

MON

TUE

WED

THU

FRI

SAT

SUN

travel
is
always
a good
IDEA

TRAVEL Information

HOTEL INFORMATION

NAME OF HOTEL:

ADDRESS:

PHONE NUMBER:

CONFIRMATION #:

RATE PER NIGHT:

FLIGHT INFORMATION

AIRLINE:

LOCATION:

FLIGHT #:

CHECK IN TIME:

DEPARTURE TIME:

REFERENCE #:

NOTES

TRAVEL Information

CAR RENTAL INFORMATION

COMPANY:

ADDRESS:

PHONE NUMBER:

CONFIRMATION #:

TOTAL COST:

EVENT INFORMATION

EVENT NAME:

LOCATION:

PHONE NUMBER:

START TIME:

OTHER:

NOTES

TRAVEL Information

HOTEL INFORMATION

NAME OF HOTEL:

ADDRESS:

PHONE NUMBER:

CONFIRMATION #:

RATE PER NIGHT:

FLIGHT INFORMATION

AIRLINE:

LOCATION:

FLIGHT #:

CHECK IN TIME:

DEPARTURE TIME:

REFERENCE #:

NOTES

Bon Voyage

TRAVEL Planner

PRE-TRAVEL CHECKLIST

1 MONTH BEFORE

2 WEEKS BEFORE

1 WEEK BEFORE

2 DAYS BEFORE

24 HOURS BEFORE

DAY OF TRAVEL

TRIP TO DO LIST Countdown

travel addict

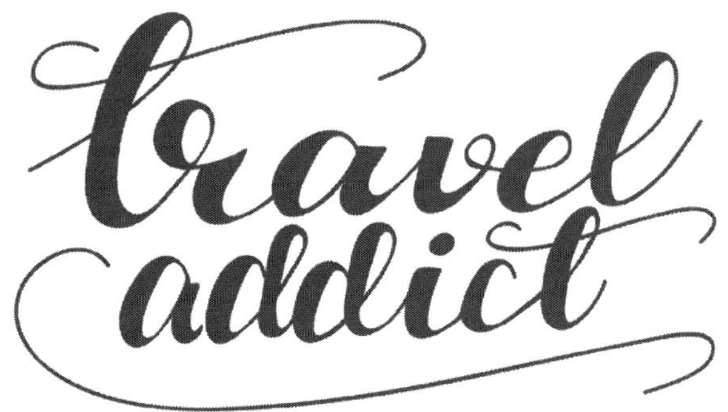

OUTFIT Planner

DAY: **DESTINATION:**   **PACKED:** ☐

DAY:

ACTIVITY: ___________________

OUTFIT: ___________________

SHOES: ___________________

ACC: ___________________

EVENING:

____

____

____

____

DAY: **DESTINATION:**   **PACKED:** ☐

DAY:

ACTIVITY: ___________________

OUTFIT: ___________________

SHOES: ___________________

ACC: ___________________

EVENING:

____

____

____

____

DAY: **DESTINATION:**   **PACKED:** ☐

DAY:

ACTIVITY: ___________________

OUTFIT: ___________________

SHOES: ___________________

ACC: ___________________

EVENING:

____

____

____

____

exiting
ADVENTURE

PACKING Check List

DOCUMENTS

- [ ] PASSPORT
- [ ] DRIVER'S LICENSE
- [ ] VISA
- [ ] PLANE TICKETS
- [ ] LOCAL CURRENCY
- [ ] INSURANCE CARD
- [ ] HEALTH CARD
- [ ] OTHER ID
- [ ] HOTEL INFORMATION
- [ ] __________________
- [ ] __________________

CLOTHING

- [ ] UNDERWEAR / SOCKS
- [ ] SWIM WEAR
- [ ] T-SHIRTS
- [ ] JEANS/PANTS
- [ ] SHORTS
- [ ] SKIRTS / DRESSES
- [ ] JACKET / COAT
- [ ] SLEEPWEAR
- [ ] SHOES
- [ ] __________________
- [ ] __________________

PERSONAL ITEMS

- [ ] SHAMPOO
- [ ] RAZORS
- [ ] COSMETICS
- [ ] HAIR BRUSH
- [ ] LIP BALM
- [ ] WATER BOTTLE
- [ ] SOAP
- [ ] TOOTHBRUSH
- [ ] JEWELRY
- [ ] __________________

ELECTRONICS

- [ ] CELL PHONE
- [ ] CHARGER
- [ ] LAPTOP
- [ ] BATTERIES
- [ ] EARPHONES
- [ ] FLASH DRIVE
- [ ] MEMORY CARD
- [ ] __________________
- [ ] __________________
- [ ] __________________

HEALTH & SAFETY

- [ ] HAND SANITIZER
- [ ] SUNSCREEN
- [ ] VITAMIN SUPPLEMENTS
- [ ] BANDAIDS
- [ ] ADVIL/TYLENOL
- [ ] CONTACTS / GLASSES
- [ ] COLD/FLU MEDS
- [ ] __________________
- [ ] __________________
- [ ] __________________

OTHER ESSENTIALS

- [ ] __________________
- [ ] __________________
- [ ] __________________
- [ ] __________________
- [ ] __________________
- [ ] __________________
- [ ] __________________
- [ ] __________________
- [ ] __________________
- [ ] __________________

PACKING Check List

OUTWARD Journey Schedule

DATE:

6

7

8

9

10

11

12

1

2

3

4

5

6

7

8

9

10

11

12

DAY:

NOTES

REMINDERS

Let's
TRAVEL
THE
World

DAILY Travel Planner

DATE:	ATTRACTION:	THINGS TO SEE

DATE:	ATTRACTION:	THINGS TO SEE

DAILY Travel Planner

DATE:	ATTRACTION:	THINGS TO SEE

DATE:	ATTRACTION:	THINGS TO SEE

Travel Expense Tracker

DESTINATION: _______________________   BUDGET GOAL: _______________________

DATE:	DESCRIPTION:	CURRENCY:	AMOUNT:

TOTAL EXPENSES:

Enjoy
every
moment

Daily TRAVEL JOURNAL

MON

TUE

WED

THU

Daily TRAVEL JOURNAL

FRI

SAT

SUN

RETURN Journey Schedule

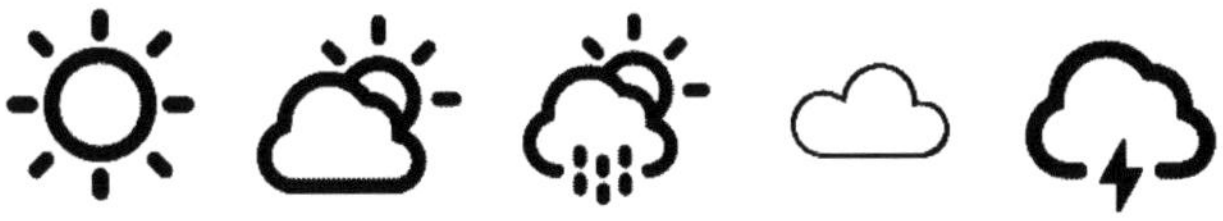

6

7

8

9

10

11

12

1

2

3

4

5

6

7

8

9

10

11

12

Made in the USA
Monee, IL
07 July 2026

56550162R00068